The Path to the Springs

*A Collection of Poems & Reflections
on Spiritual Refreshment*

Debra Boggs Saunders

McClain Printing Company
Parsons, WV
www.mcclainprinting.com
2009

International Standard Book Number 0-87012-792-6
Printed in the United States of America
Copyright © 2009 by Debra Saunders
Little Creak, LLC
Leesburg, VA
All Rights Reserved
2009

This book is dedicated to my parents,
Rev. Doyal and Jenivieve Cruikshank,
who led by example,
and in spite of the circumstances,
always believed for the best.

Credits

I give thanks for all those who have helped me and supported my efforts in writing this book. There is no way I can fully thank you. Please know that you are loved and appreciated.

The beautiful photos used in and throughout this book are the work of Lisa Boggs. All the photos contained herein are the copyrighted property of Lisa Boggs, Lisa Boggs Photography (www.lisaboggsphotography.com).

Thanks to my daughter, Laura Burhenn, for proofing and editing the poems, as well as designing the book cover. I cannot thank Laura enough for her support, ideas, and obvious love she gave to this work.

I would also like to thank the following who have supported me in this work: my husband, John; my sister, Ann; my sixth grade teacher and inspiration, Mrs. Jean Dransfield; my Aunt Jean Boggs, who gave me the idea for the printer, McClain Publishing; my Aunt Janet Boggs Crisco, who valued and encouraged the idea of the work as a part of the "journey through life;" to all of my friends who have labored through this part of my journey with me; and to God, the Creator, who gives to all.

I can only pray that the love that has gone into this book will manifest itself to those who read and share it.

Thank you all.

Forward

On a clear day in June 2008, I journeyed to Berkeley Springs, West Virginia. For some time, I had a vision to visit there. The vision was simple: In it, I saw shops and shopkeepers, and a few of my African American sisters brightly arrayed and gracefully walking down the street. The mountains provided the backdrop for the springs and those I might meet there. And the ancient and lasting springs themselves, the constant symbol of all that is new and fresh.

For me, Berkeley Springs always held special memories. In my childhood, it was a place of magic. For these and other reasons the journey is now – and will remain – a touchstone to recalling the things that bring true refreshment to us as we progress along the pathways of our lives.

Should your path in life bring you to the springs, you may be carried through countryside and along mountains. Or you may travel through the valley, bridge the gap, cross the river. Approach the area surrounding the springs and stop by the pools. You may bring your cup to the fountain. Take time to fill your cup and be refreshed before you continue on.

The springs at Berkeley Springs have been there for a long, long time. How many have been there before you is unknown. But if you travel there and drink from the water, you will share in the experience of all those who have gone before.

Go now, along your own journey. And embrace the things that bring real refreshment and joy to your life.

Meditation I

Meditation for this day:

Breathe deeply.

And do not forget to recall

how wonderful it is to breathe.

Today

Today I ran away

To see the sky and

View the mountains.

As I saw them

And embraced

What life had given me this day,

I realized I had not run away at all –

I had only come home.

The Highway

And when I travel the highway

And pass the unknown road,

It calls to me like an old friend

And bids me to

Come and share

In the fellowship

Berkeley Springs

Today I walked in Berkeley Springs.

I saw where Washington imbibed the waters for his health; I walked where he walked and saw where he bathed in the healing springs.

I had often pictured myself traveling to Berkeley Springs to walk past art shops and eateries; in my thoughts, I had overlooked history.

My awareness was focused on people I might meet and how we might interact. A time for sharing.

I pictured my black sisters walking in bright dresses, heads held high – graceful and sure.

My sisters were the art.

When I walked, I was not disappointed: my sisters and a brother stood with me.

They were the art.

We met, we spoke, we laughed.
We breathed in life as one.

The grass and the daisy

The blade of grass grows tall and stretches toward the sky.

It does not move, except the wind stirs it a little.

It opens itself to soothing rain.

In wonder, it observes the unfolding of its sister the daisy.

America

Unduplicatable

Though others may try.

Yes, we have made our mistakes;

But we press on.

Do not look back we implore –

Put your hand to the plow and toil on.

James Anderson Boggs and Susan Cutlip Boggs

Upon visiting the grave site where they are laid
Gassaway, WV
July 8, 2008

Solemn and staid

Working hard, Cultivating land;
Hands hold hands;

Hands are holding other hands.
Side by side they pull the plow.

With money earned, they buy oxen to work their land.

Managing meager means, they produce and multiply.

Susan and James, together they face the question and answer
the country divided.

Hearts are broken when closer
Still, the other relatives cannot decide the question for
themselves.

Will they side with friends, kin and countrymen?
Who is their neighbor?

Deep sighs; eyes dry, then flowing: death has knocked at their
door.

Eyes lifted to God, and shovels turned into the earth –
Search to find a meeting place that will explain the hearts
divided.
Into twilight, eyes fixed, unyielding

They remain together in life,
And they succumb together in eternal rest,
Still together,
Side by side.

Helen, now on the hill

Many years ago, I have heard, Helen was my Brother's Mother.

Helen, the picture of loveliness, gave birth to my body.

In pictures, we are frail and pained.

To remember Helen is difficult, for me, one so young.

My Brother may remember.

My Brother may remember – laughter, singing, crying.

My Brother may remember Helen. She kissed him one night. Then she did not come back.

Where, he may ask, did she go?

I could not remember seeing her.

Until yesterday.

No, I did not catch a glimpse of her, but I found a sign, a marker, which bore her name – indicating that spot where she might stay, if she wanted.

When she went to that spot in a wooded glen on a hillside high above the winding road, she would not know it would become a noisy highway in some years.

Helen may have thought the hillside to be a peaceful place, many years prior.

But now, when asked, *Where is Helen?* One may answer: *Helen, now on the hill.*

I don't think the cars on the road below are aware.

A few years ago, Hugh Boggs, Jr., decided he would visit Helen, now on the hill.

I wonder what he thought of the spot, now with whizzing cars below.

I wonder what the tiny frogs think of the hillside. I wonder if the birds think that Helen, now on the hill, has found the clarity she wanted.

My favorite things

Excerpt from a letter written February 9, 2009

- Nothing is like the smell and texture of a sweet ripe peach. And who can match a homegrown tomato in season?

- The first warm morning of spring – when you feel the season has passed from coldness

- The first few clear frosty nights of fall, when the world takes on a new perspective, clean and clear

- The morning when you get up, following a beautiful snowfall, and nothing is moving – just quiet stillness – no wind, no cars, no planes, no animal noises – just quiet stillness

- The end of August into September, with the sound of crickets and lazy feel of sunshine, and the rhythm as you can almost sense the grasses begin to wind down their growing season, and insects in the field make a final surge to be heard and recognized before the weather turns

- The distinct sound of a waterfall, hearing it first and then seeing it later

- Sitting as a child, in the semi-darkness in front of the Christmas tree, with only the lights of the tree to see, smelling the fragrance of the evergreen, and dreaming only the thoughts of a child as you behold the sight in awe and wonderment

- Hearing the story of the birth of the Christ child and holding a star or reciting a verse for a play, or beholding the procession of the three Wise Men in your mind's eye, as they followed the Star to the Stable

- Hearing the story where there is no room in the Inn for the Mother of the baby Jesus – thinking as a child, "What does this mean?" and later experiencing times as an adult when you experienced times when there was no room in the Inn for you

- Coming to the realization as an adult that getting the "No Room in the Inn" response may feel sad at the time, but then later, life brings other Blessings; God makes a way.

When it looked as if I did not have a Mother, God provided an Excellent Mother who Loved me like her very own. When it looked as if I did not have a Father who could care for me, God provided an Excellent Father who Loved me like his very own. When it looked as if I did not know anyone when we moved, God provided true friends who loved, and loved, and loved.

These are the things that are special to me – what is life without friends?

I learned long ago it is the people who make life special. You have made my life and the lives of my family infinitely special.

God has granted me excellent gifts – great friends and meaningful memories.

You are the gift

I am my gift of what I bring. The bread I make, the salad I take, the tea I share, I am in the gift and I am the gift.

My hug, my touch, my care, my joy, my longing, my advent into the life of others; these are my gifts. I and my gifts are one. I cannot be separated from the oneness of the love I offer to my fellow being.

What you bring is your gift. You are the gift you bring. Do not hesitate to bring your gift joyfully.

You are the gift. Relish what you have to offer. Do not compare your gift to others. Your gift is yours alone.

See the gift you bring for what it is. See your gift for who you are.

You are the gift, and the world responds.

Meditation II

Meditation for this day:

Once you have found yourself, do not let yourself go.

God Exists

God Exists. I know it.

And I am glad.

Some people question or debate the existence of God. Not me.

And I am glad.

I think of it like this: God has done all the big stuff. He hung the stars in the sky. He created a big light for the day and a smaller orb for the night.

Lightning, thunder, rain, food, laughter... God thought of it all.

Think of it: Polar bears, cheetahs, cats, mice, dogs, leopards, snakes, elephants, zebras, bees, honey, clover, fish, trees, rocks, streams, springs, waterfalls, seas, turtles, gophers, and yes, even skunks.

I can't think of too many things that God left out. (Actually, I can't think of anything.)

And what is there for us to do?

We are supposed to enjoy it.

And, Oh yes – we are supposed to love each other.

It sounds like God had the hard part.

If we could just learn to enjoy everything and stop trying to mess things up…

I am going to work on my part now.

Thank you, God, for going to all this trouble just for us.

In praise of all things not performed by committee

Stars shining in the heavens brightly and without number
The crescent moon in the harvest season
The moon full and radiant in the cold December night

The symphony of the crickets on a late summer afternoon
The stamp and snort of the mighty stallion standing watch
          over mares and foal
The lowing of cattle, reddish brown and white-faced, in
          the early, snow-covered morning

Sounds of the rushing water and the tumbling splashing
          waterfall
Fall leaves blowing and spinning in a silent whirlwind on
          a deserted country road
Lightning splitting the summer night before the
          unleashing of rain

The mountain goat standing on the pointed rock, unaware
          of the yawning chasm beneath
Black and white cattle chewing cud complacently in lush
          green meadows
The solitary leap of a rainbow trout in an icy mountain
          stream

The shiny green barbed leaves of the holly tree protecting
          the bright red berries
The arc of the sun upon the desert as it releases
          shimmering waves of air
The innocent, watching, unwavering dark eyes of the
          resting baby seal

The playful nipping of puppies with razor sharp teeth
Kittens in cashmere-like coats, softly nesting with their

mother
Young colts frolicking with pure pleasure on over-sized
        legs

The hairy rough brown of coconut skin covering the
        smooth white flesh and milk within
The undulating flight of the Brown Pelican skimming,
        single file over beach cottage and sand in the low-
        country morning
The snowy white crane resting in its one legged pose in the
        lowland marsh

Driving sleet, snow and ice covering the woolen head and
        shoulders of the American Bison, hiding matted
        furry patchwork underneath
The zoo elephant sitting awkwardly, trunk lifted, hide
        hanging heavy, thick and grey, smeared and muddied
The rubbery slippery dolphin dancing unchoreographed
        on the surface of the blue-gray Atlantic

The alligator, log-like and submerged just below the
        surface of muddy water, lurking and warming in the sun
The great and giant moss-laden oaks of Savannah,
        standing as silent sentinels, extending outstretched
        limbs to the sky, while holding firmly to the earth
        beneath
The crossing currents of the sea, swift and deadly,
        recording silently off-shore passings of ships and
        crew, unsuccessful in the voyage

The formal march of Penguins, arriving in stiff suits to
        their pre-appointed meeting place
The shape shifting spring flight of Canadian Geese
        honking rhythmically in midair
The telltale white flash of the leaping deer as it disappears
        into the tangled thicket

The deafening crash of waves onto the shore
The circling, screaming seagulls
The scattering of seashells on the beach at low tide

All these and other acts being performed without prior
request or approval by committee.

The Tree

Observe the Tree,

Robed in majesty

Whether with leaves

Or bare.

Falling Leaves

In spring, the trees are surprised to see developing buds on their branches.

Like teenagers, budding with youth and enthusiasm, they grow and develop, all without a wish or a thought to make it happen.

Spring rains feed the trees.

Buds develop into leaves, some green, some yellowish, some with reds and blue hues.

Some even surprise themselves with flowering masses, like parade goers in bright and brilliant frocks: white or pink or magenta or creamy laces that float on light breezes.

Summer may see the flowers come and go, see the leaves grow larger.

Suddenly the trees feel grown up and have confidence the leaves will be theirs forever.

The birds, and squirrels arrive to take a spot and stake a claim where they want to plant their nest and welcome their young, see them flourish as nature decrees.

The trees stand strong and commit to their growth.

Fall may see ferocious rains and driving winds fling leaves of brown, red, orange, and yellow into today's earth or lift them up into tomorrow.

I walk among the leaves and wonder from whence they came.

I wonder about their journey what wind brought them to where they now lay.

Will the leaves stay here?

Will the wind blow them further, scattering them once more? Will the rake move the leaves, pulling them into piles for fire and ash? Or will the leaves be used for bedding and comfort for animals? Or a pile for children to play?

These leaves, I walk among them. I savor the shapes, the textures, the colors, the hues, the sizes and the handy work of One who is greater than I.

From where they come, from trees they have sprung, from the journeys they have taken, they are here now, and I walk among them.

What journeys brought them to this place, I do not know. But they are here now and I stand with them.

Tree rings

Rings of the tree
Indicate years and seasons of growth
The inner rings represent beginning and youth
The outer rings represent maturity and growth

It is hard to count the rings of a tree until it has been cut

We have rings of growth that may be harder to count

Even if we are cut, it is hard for us to count the rings of
growth we have experienced

Growing into ourselves may take time

Some rings, we think, may take much longer than others

Some rings may be hard for us to see, as the rings are invisible
to ourselves and visible to others

Some rings may be hard for others to see, as the rings are
invisible to others but visible to ourselves

Some rings are very round and regular

Some rings are more like amoeboid markers

All rings take time and all rings grow outward

Grow beyond yourself

Grace

The graceful bird rises, floats, descends

And amazes all who see it.

It needs no lessons

Or help

From any man.

Undiscovered Colours

On the sand, the water comes in,
Goes out, falls backwards, rolls forward, first lazily,
Then slapping the shore,
Then splashing, and sliding forward, then backward.

The plane of sand sparkles, glints,
Extends toward land and
Falls away beneath the waves –

Sand, sea, shells, stones – gifts from the water,
Left for us to enjoy and savour.

The light plays off the shells, and the
Glint of the sun
Produces colours
That to me
Have been undiscovered
Until now.

Like a secret code of life, the shell, water, sand & sun
Conspire to illuminate colours
That flash, swell, shine and fade.

When I attempt to retrieve
And hold the colours –
These colours as yet undiscovered –
Cannot be held captive
And are unable to be reproduced
Or engineered.

Because these colours
Like the secrets of life
Are undiscovered;

And upon closer inspection,
Remain the same.

Meditation III

Meditation for this day:

I will trust fully in the Lord

Now

You are special now
God has made you in a special way
You are special
Now is the time to know
How special you are.
Yes, you are special now.
And remember,
It is always now.

Building Bridges

Going through life and seeing needs
Refusing to know who it is
Call the name and label the person
Stand and look away

Know differences and point them out
Collect rocks and throw them at offenders
Or better yet
Build a wall

This way you will never have to know your neighbor
And you will never know yourself.

Take the stones and mix some mortar
Learn to arch and flex and sway
Place the stones across and forward.

Find the spot to move together
Find the things that make you laugh
Live the laughter, keep on moving
Toward yourself at last.

Find yourself and make some changes
Love your neighbor as yourself
Break the fences, cast them under
Love the moment, free at last.

Building bridges tie the wounded
Building bridges find the truth
Holding in the framework ever
Hope for love and hope for peace.

Bridgework ties our lives together

Brings us toward the light of soul
Bridges span the arch of difference
Pull our spirits within reach.

The speck of sand

I stand on the shore, a speck of sand;

I face the vastness of the ocean

And wonder at the tides that moved me to this spot.

I face the East, thinking of others: shifting, being shifted,
being pulled by the tide and the foaming waves.

I marvel at those who have traveled from other shores, and
are now beside me on this shore.

Some are warming in the sun; others are in the ebb and flow
of the early morning tide, going gently back and forth, back
and forth, back and forth, back and forth; others are on the
mantle of the ocean, the ledge of the deep, pondering the
great abyss.

Fall into the abyss; plunge into the abyss; become aware that
you have become the abyss.

Days pass, months go by, a year or two has turned into a
decade.

Suddenly you are on the shore, on a land distant from where
you began, now suddenly familiar. You are warmed on shore
and joined by others.
Together you form the coast.

You stand with each other and bow to each other and
embrace each other and realize you are not alone.

No time to be afraid

No time to be afraid
Stand on up and move on down;
No time to be afraid
Square your shoulders,
Raise your head.

Stand strong and move on out.

Stand strong and move on out.

No Bargaining

There are no ways to bargain with God.

Though many try,
They fall short.

You may find that
Bargaining with God
Leaves little response.

Most who have given the effort
Have discovered God has the upper hand.
It becomes evident they lack
Leverage to sway God with bargaining.

Bargaining may be better left to unions, to agents,
to buyers and sellers.

Another way to gain
God's attention
Might be to ask –
Asking God might be better
Than bargaining.

To ask humbly might be better than
To demand
In anger.

Demanding may not be the most useful
Way to approach God... Though
It is still used
By many.

Even better than bargaining, asking, or demanding might be
Listening

To God.

Maybe God is not so open to a
Conversation with
Someone who is not willing to hear
His side and His thoughts.

I know I find it hard to hear what
Anyone is saying if I speak
Over their words.

But I do think there is
Room for a conversation
And in any good conversation,
Somebody has to listen.

I hope God has something to say to me.

I hope that He thinks enough of me to have something
To tell me. And I hope when I respond, He will listen.

I hope there is enough for a full conversation.

I am going to go clean my ears now,
Just in case.

Meditation IV

Meditation for this day:

I will take the next step by faith.

Excessive
December 5, 2008

I know my Savior's Love is for me so excessive

He Loves me and He holds my hand,
He hears me when I pray.

I know my Savior's love is for me so excessive.

He holds me and He leads me on,
He's with me Everyday.

Chorus
Well, He is my Rock my Sword my Shield, He hears me
when I pray.
He holds my hand and heals with love, He will not stray
away.

Well, I know my Savior's Love is for me so excessive:
There is no End to His Great Love, He's with me every day.

(Repeat main verse and chorus)

Out of many voices
Written for my daughter Laura, 2009

[Make your music.
Make your music and make your mark.
Make sure that you are making time to leave this legacy
of what is truly, only yours.
Make no apologies for you who are
only make your way into the music,
as the music makes it way through you.]

Out of many voices, one voice
rises to the heavens.
As it drifts upward, floats outward, it suddenly spins its way
back to earth,
where uplifted ears, eyes, and hearts are now aware of the
voice,
as if hearing it, seeing it and feeling it for the first time...
the voice grows stronger, clearer, and more vibrant until it is
part of eternity, and the people feel the ageless pulse.

Lift your voice within and let it flow and resonate
like crystal waterfalls that spring forth from within
and never tire of flowing.

Out of the many voices, believe that your voice is the
purposed one, and let it go freely and unrestrained to your
brothers and sisters of this age and throughout eternity. Let it
be as it is intended. Let it flow without remorse. Let it be as
sweet waters from the spring of eternity, from a realm where
no one can cease the flow.

Out of many voices one will shine forth as the one sent to be heard. Let your heart sing with joy, and joy in the singing. Others will hear the song and marvel in its wholeness.

Lift your voice and your voice will lift the world.

My sisters and I are One

My sisters and I are One

Our hues and shapes and tones are not who we are

Our burdens are not who we are

Our shortcomings are not who we are.

My sisters and I are One.

If one has a burden, the burden is our burden.

If one has a blessing, the blessing is our blessing.

If one has learned some wisdom, the wisdom is our wisdom.

My sisters and I are One

Our hopes should bind us closer and build the sisterhood

Our dreams should be shared and celebrated and sustained together.

My sisters and I are One.

We seek the bridge of connectivity and see the wall as a divide.

I can meet my sisters at the wall, and when I do, we will stand on the same side of the wall and wail together, holding hands, and lifting our prayers as One.

My sisters and I are One.

We will eat of the bread of life together and breathe in life together and praise our Creator with One voice.

My sisters and I are One in the spirit and our souls sing in unison and our voices resonate Together.

I shall never cease to give Thanks because

My sisters and I are One.

Which day

Which day will I pick to leave?

On my best day.

One day, I will have the day that cannot be improved upon.

It may be a surprise to me, or it may be known.

When I have had the perfect day, I will think,
This could be the day. I have never had a better day.

Wouldn't this be a great day to exit: going out on the high note?

But when that day comes, I may never know.

What if I could live every day like it is the perfect day?

If every day is the perfect day, then every day could be the
day when I might leave.

I want to live simply.

One great day… I will take my flight.

Flight without wings -- when I am at last free from this body,
which has served me for so long.

When the form I am becomes formless – *I shall know as I am
known.*